Life Lessons

of the

Good Teacher

McDougal & Associates

Servants of Christ and Stewards of the
Mysteries of God

Life Lessons

of the

Good Teacher

Overcoming Life's Obstacles:
The Wilderness Season

Stephanie S. Johnson, M.Ed.

Published by:

McDougal & Associates
18896 Greenwell Springs Road
Greenwell Springs, LA 70739
www.thepublishedword.com

McDougal & Associates is an organization dedicated to
spreading the Gospel of the Lord Jesus Christ to as many
people as possible in the shortest time possible.

ISBN: 978-1-940461-72-4

Printed on demand in the U.S., the U.K. and Australia
For Worldwide Distribution

Dedication

I dedicate this book:

First and foremost, to my Lord and Savior, Jesus Christ.

To my Mom, I love you. You've always been there for me. I thank you for the impact you have made on my life. Dad (now deceased), I love you and miss you.

To my daughters, Danielle Faith and Chanelle Hope, you are EVERYTHING! I love you both with all my heart and am very proud of you both. You are beautiful young ladies. I declare that you will manifest your purpose and destiny in life. You are continually blessed.

To my brothers and sister and the rest of my family, I pray God's richest blessings upon you and your families. Be blessed!

Contents

Foreword by
Apostle Reggie Wilson

It is amazing how we sometimes meet people in passing and then later really get to know them. That's my story with Stephanie Johnson, this exciting woman of God, a woman who loves the Lord and loves people of all kinds. Writing her foreword wasn't hard because I've had the pleasure of developing a great relationship with her over many years. She knows how to put her foot down and set her face like a flint when she believes that the Father has spoken.

This book is a testimony of someone who has been on a journey, and Stephanie's teaching skills have afforded her the ability to communicate a long-overdue message. I read the manuscript a couple of times and truly felt that it represented a new beginning for her, one that would present a challenge to others to listen more closely to life's lessons and cash them in for future success.

Life Lessons of the Good Teacher is a pleasant read. It unfolds both scriptural content and personal experiences that are honest. It will challenge those who have discovered that life brings us all a wilderness experience, and it may occur more than once on the route to your destiny. Reading and digesting this book will help you process the good, bad and ugly you encounter along the way, accepting the reality that once your attitude and your faith align with the promises of God, nothing will be impossible for you. You will begin to see gradual and sometimes miraculous interventions as you learn that the wilderness is necessary to prepare you for your best days. Trust me, this is a great book to have as you navigate to your new frontier.

Without giving away too much, let me say this: Pastor Stephanie Johnson has "spilled the beans," so to speak, in *Life Lessons of the Good Teacher*. Each chapter contains valuable nuggets of truth. She shows us that seeing things from God's perspective is guaranteed to benefit us in the end, and each of these lessons come from her own wilderness experiences.

I encourage and admonish you to read this book with an open heart and a willingness to work out your own salvation. In it, the author asks and answers such important questions as:

- Do I shortcut the process or do I trust God to use it to make me a better person?
- Will I complain or will I learn to give the Lord praise?
- Should I submit or should I keep on running, using my own strength?

All of this and more awaits you in *Life Lessons of the Good Teacher*, a book written in a most appropriate season. While all around us is madness, hurt and uncertainty of what comes next in life, Stephanie gives us a book full of lessons to encourage us not to give up but to go on through.

Thank you, Pastor. From a father's heart to a spiritual daughter, you have blessed many, and you will continue, through this book, to do so. I am truly proud of you and this work!

Apostle Dr. Reggie Wilson

Introduction

Throughout the text, you will notice these little wisdom nuggets. They're my way of guiding you through the text in order to make certain that the message is clear to you.

It may be helpful to take notes as you travel through the book. You'll find tips to help you through your daily walk with God.

I am writing this book from a personal perspective, high-lighting different times in my life when I had to practice encouraging myself to walk as an overcomer and to know that I could *"do all things through Christ that strengthens me"* as the Bible promises.

Stephanie S. Johnson, M.Ed.
New Orleans, Louisiana

Life Lesson 1

The Wilderness

This book is for people who are coming out of their wilderness season and entering into their destiny and divine purpose in life. It's for people who have been called and appointed by God, children of God who haven't quit in the midst of the storm, prayer warriors who prayed and fought through the onslaught of the enemy and the cares of this life.

When you hear the word *wilderness*, you might think of a land where there is no water, no food, a dry and harsh environment. True, the wilderness may be all of that in the natural, but more than anything, it is spiritual appointment that every believer and every child of God must visit in order to experience God in a way that reveals His presence in your life. It is this presence that comes to give you the victory over death, Hell and the grave. He ushers in Holy Ghost power and the ability to speak the Word of God, so that you are able to resist temptation and walk in victory.

No one is exempt from the wilderness. If Jesus, the Son of God, who was man and God simultaneously, had to endure a wilderness season, then we must all go through that proving time. The wilderness is a place of humility, edification, chastisement, preparation and disrobing before God. It is an experience that every man and woman is called to face and overcome.

The wilderness is a time of letting go of self, calling on God and welcoming His presence; a time of chastening that will lead you to renewal and favor. The wilderness is a place where God hides His face and you press through the fog of everyday life issues to find His presence (see Psalm 27). God purposely hides His face so that we will seek Him.

Webster's Dictionary defines the word *wilderness* as: "1. A tract or region uncultivated and uninhabited by human beings 2. An area essentially undisturbed by human activity, together with its naturally developed life community b: an empty or pathless area or region." Spiritually, the wilderness is a place of emptiness and starvation. It is a place of testing and revelation, where one can see who they really are in the flesh and must make a choice between God or the ways of the flesh. It is a time of transition and movement toward God's perfect will for your life. God becomes your personal Life Coach because He sees your desire to serve Him. He has to usher you into a time of solitude so that you can understand the purpose and call on your life. When you have mastered what you have been taught, you will be equipped with wisdom and power.

You must understand that the enemy will come to tempt you in the wilderness. His goal is to ultimately destroy you. But when you take hold of God the Father as your Refuge, you will not be defeated. Instead, you will come out of the fire refined as pure gold, just as Jesus did when He experienced His wilderness season.

The Scriptures say in Matthew 4:1-11:

> *Then was Jesus led up of the Spirit into the wilderness to be tempted of the devil. And when he had fasted forty days and forty nights, he was afterward an hungered. And when the tempter came to him, he said, If thou be the Son of God, command that these stones be made bread.*
>
> *But he answered and said, It is written, Man shall not live by bread alone, but by every word that proceedeth out of the mouth of God.*
>
> *Then the devil taketh him up into the holy city, and setteth him on a pinnacle of the temple, and saith unto him, If thou be the Son of God, cast thyself down: for it is written, He shall give his angels charge concerning thee: and in their hands they shall bear thee up, lest at any time thou dash thy foot against a stone.*
>
> *Jesus said unto him, It is written again, Thou shalt not tempt the Lord thy God.*

Again, the devil taketh him up into an exceeding high mountain, and sheweth him all the kingdoms of the world, and the glory of them; and saith unto him, All these things will I give thee, if thou wilt fall down and worship me.

Then saith Jesus unto him, Get thee hence, Satan: for it is written, Thou shalt worship the Lord thy God, and him only shalt thou serve.

Then the devil leaveth him, and, behold, angels came and ministered unto him.

After you have done everything you know how to do in your own strength and you have run out of strength, you open your spirit to receive because you are tired and at a point of desperation.

Psalm 37:23-24 (NKJV) states:

The steps of a good man are ordered by the LORD, and He delights in his way. Though he fall, he shall not be utterly cast down; for the LORD upholds him with His hand.

Did you know that your steps are ordered by God? That means that God is the One who leads and guides you into His will. You don't just stumble into it. God leads you into the wilderness, just as He did Jesus, so that He could prepare Him for ministry. The Father needed Jesus to see that

The Wilderness

He had the power to resist the enemy by using the Word to gain victory over the plan of the enemy. Likewise, the Father ushers you into that wilderness place so that you might realize that the power of God is in you, and you have the ability to resist Satan and all of his temptations by speaking the Word of God to him. When you do this, Satan has no choice but to flee.

There will be suffering and tribulations as we walk this walk in the wilderness, but the Bible says, in 1 Peter 5:10:

> *But the God of all grace, who hath called us unto his eternal glory by Christ Jesus, after that ye have suffered a while, make you perfect, stablish, strengthen, settle you.*

Now, the Father becomes the Potter, and you are the clay. He can finally make you into what He planned for your life before your conception. No more beating at the wind or wrestling the waves, for God is in control. Now He can allow you to walk in the destiny that He called you into ten, twenty, or even thirty or more years ago. You are now ready for God to use you in the fullness to His glory.

When you are in the wilderness, it is a time of consecration. Just as Jesus fasted for forty days and forty nights, you, the believer, should have times of fasting, prayer and reading the Word in the presence of God. Yours may not be a forty-day fast like Jesus'; it may be only two or three days (done on a regular basis) of being shut in with God in order to bring the flesh under subjection. Only you know how long and what is required in your wilderness season.

During that time of consecration, it is important to seek God's will and direction for your life. Keep a journal of what God speaks to you daily. If you don't hear God speaking, you are not at the point of breakthrough yet, and you must continue to press in until God begins to reveal Himself to you.

You might say, "I can't tell if God is speaking to me or not." I would answer: If your heart is tuned in to God, you will hear His voice. God is all-powerful, and He will teach you how to commune with Him.

The Scriptures say, in Psalm 46:10-11:

> *Be still, and know that I am God: I will be exalted among the heathen, I will be exalted in the earth. The LORD hosts is with us; the God of Jacob is our refuge. Selah.*

This means that if you allow God to do it, He will show you who He is and will manifest Himself in your life in all of His glory.

Because you work every day and go about the daily business of taking care of family, home and finances, it may be difficult for you to be shut in for long periods of time to seek God. As you go about your daily routines, set aside specific times in your schedule to meet God. Your appointed time in the wilderness doesn't stop because you have to go to work, take care of children or pay bills. Life as you know it must go on. Therefore, you must consciously make God a priority and use wisdom in yielding your flesh to Him even as you "do life."

Designate a time that is just for communication with the Father, your own special prayer time. This may have to be in the evening after the rest of the family is asleep, or it can be early in the morning when the house is still quiet. Find what works for you, and make that your designated time with the Father.

As you enter into that time every day, you will find that it gets easier and easier to feel God's presence with you. He will transform you as you seek His presence, and He will give you power to resist any temptations and cast off any weights that are coming against you.

Psalm 4:3-4 says:

> *But know that the LORD set apart him that is godly for himself: the LORD will hear when I call unto him. Stand in awe, and sin not: commune with your own heart upon your bed, and be still. Selah.*

In other words, it is God who has ordained that you are "set apart" just for Him. You are ordained to spend time with Him in His presence seeking His face, seeking His guidance, seeking all that He has to offer His child.

It is written, in 1 Corinthian 2:9:

> *Eye hath not seen, nor ear heard, neither have entered into the heart of man, the things which God hath prepared for them that love him.*

Child of God, these are the benefits of serving God, realizing that you are His and that you have been bought with a price.

Let me offer some clarification about the wilderness: you may have more than one wilderness season in your lifetime. This is not a once-in-a-lifetime thing. When the Father sees that you have need of a time of refreshing (because the cares of this life and daily trials are weakening you, and you are confused and need new direction), He will nudge you into another time of solitude in which you will have to seek Him. Even after experiencing great moves of God (in which it seems that nothing can go wrong), you will find that you are in need of a private encounter with Him, to get you back on track, clear the confusion and renew your vision for the future.

There will always be something new to learn or to experience that requires a wilderness period, and the Lord will lead you into that experience in order to get your attention, so that He can equip you and strengthen you for what lies just ahead.

Remember, Jesus was led into the wilderness very soon after He was baptized by John the Baptist and was validated by the Father. The Scriptures say, in Matthew 3:17:

> *And lo a voice came from heaven, saying, This is my beloved Son, in whom I am well pleased.*

Yes, Jesus was validated by the Father at His baptism, and shortly thereafter He was led into the wilderness to be tempted by the devil in order to prepare Him for His earthly ministry. The point is this: Just because God validates who you are and sets His approval upon you does not mean that you can say, "Let the good times roll." It doesn't mean smooth sailing from here on out. It doesn't mean you have arrived at your destination and are perfect because God is pleased with you. It simply means that you have been anointed, appointed and called by God, and now He can use you for His glory as you walk further into your destiny.

Yes, there will be good times, moments when you see the glory of God manifested; but there will also be times when you will wonder, *Where is God?* All in all, you will just know that He is with you and that He will never leave you nor forsake you.

You should read the rest of this book only if you believe that you are ready to allow God to have His way in your life.

You have walked through the place of learning to surrender to God. You have discovered that without Him you can do nothing. It's in Him that we live and move and have our being. So, you realize that your days of isolation, wandering, confusion, hopelessness and bewilderment are fading. The end of the wilderness season is near. Prepare to come out.

In preparation, take off the wilderness wardrobe, remove the sad countenance, get rid of the froward mouth, cast off your load of depression and that spirit of heaviness.

There are many lessons to be learned from spending time in the wilderness. In the wilderness, you may feel alone, cast away from God's presence, but your spirit knows that God is there. Your spirit knows that He will never leave you nor forsake you. At the same time, your soul wonders, "Why did God not reveal Himself more quickly in my time of trouble?" You mind thinks, "If only I could feel His presence like before, if only I could go back and change my actions and my ways." But know that this is a valley you must pass through in order to know God in a deeper way. So, you cry out, "Lord, don't take your Holy Spirit from me."

The wilderness equips you for rejection, failure and loss. It teaches you how to be abased and how to abound. It helps you to let go of old habits, old friends, old places and old thoughts. In the wilderness, you are able to take off the grave clothes that have kept you bound and to be washed of the scent of sin and defeat. The wilderness brings you to a place of willingness to be obedient, looking ahead, hoping and trusting in God.

Coming out of the wilderness causes you to remember the promise you received before you entered the wilderness and why you had to go there. You suddenly realize that if you had kept doing what you were doing, you would keep getting the same result, for God will never change His stance. What He said shall come to pass. Therefore, it is up to you to work out your own soul salvation, even if it means spending extra time in the wilderness. Let that be your decision.

Don't be like the children of Israel. They had to wander around the wilderness for forty years, wasting time and their destiny, because of an unrepentant heart and their disobedience. Know that the wilderness has a purpose, but then accomplish that purpose as quickly as possible and get ready to come out of the wilderness into your ultimate destiny.

Are you ready to put on the joy of your salvation and walk in the newness of life and rejoice in the Lord? He has caused you to triumph in your proving season. Now serve Him with gladness.

In this book, I refer to my journeys and wilderness experiences as "Life Lessons," lessons I've learned as I walked with God throughout the years, and it is now my joy to share those lessons with you.

A *lesson* is defined as "an amount of teaching given at one time; a period of learning or teaching, to instruct or teach." By profession, I am a teacher, and I can say, without a doubt, that I have learned more lessons spiritually than I have ever been able to teach others.

When Jesus walked on the earth, He used parables to teach His disciples. According *Webster's Dictionary*, a *parable* is "a short story that teaches a moral or spiritual lesson." Another dictionary defines *parable* as "a simple story used to illustrate a moral or spiritual lesson, as told by Jesus in the Gospels." Jesus had a strategy to get His point across to His leaders and to His people because He was and is the Master Teacher. Glory to His name!

The Bible states, in Matthews 13:10-17:

> *And the disciples came, and said unto him, Why speakest thou unto them in parables?*
> *He answered and said unto them, Because it is given unto you to know the mysteries of the kingdom of heaven, but to them it is not given. For whosoever hath, to him shall be given, and he shall have more abundance: but whosoever hath not, from him shall be taken away even that he hath. Therefore speak I to them in parables: because they seeing see not; and hearing they hear not, neither do they understand. And in them is fulfilled the prophecy of Esaias, which saith, By hearing ye shall hear, and shall not understand; and seeing ye shall see, and shall not perceive: for this people's heart is waxed gross, and their ears are*

dull of hearing, and their eyes they have closed; lest at any time they should see with their eyes and hear with their ears, and should understand with their heart, and should be converted, and I should heal them.

But blessed are your eyes, for they see: and your ears, for they hear. For verily I say unto you, That many prophets and righteous men have desired to see those things which ye see, and have not seen them; and to hear those things which ye hear, and have not heard them.

Wow, that's a mouthful! Here is what I have gleaned about why Jesus used parables:

1. He taught using parables to make His message clear to everyone. However, the full meaning was revealed only to those who loved Him and desired to do His will.
2. He used parables to relate to both the common people and the religious leaders of His day. Instead of using scholarly words, He spoke in everyday language.
3. Matthew 7:28-29 states, *"And it came to pass, when Jesus had ended these sayings, the people were astonished at his doctrine: for he taught them as one having authority, and not as the scribes."* So, Jesus used the parables to set Himself apart from the religious leaders of the

day who used long passages of the Law and traditions to support their message.

4. Jesus spoke in parables because they were part of the culture of the day. Storytelling was a way of life back then. He used His parables to personally connect with the people on their level. The parables had spiritual meaning and purpose.

5. Jesus used the parables as a tool to reveal the Messiah, assert His authority and reach those who were ready to hear.

Just as Jesus used His parables, I will use my "Life Lessons" to reveal what I feel God is saying for His people today. These lessons that may not seem super-deep or super-spiritual, but they can set you on the right course to see God in a way you have never seen Him before.

LIFE LESSON 1
SELF-CHECK

Think about a time when you felt like you were in a wilderness season. How did you handle it? Was it one of those times when you cracked under the pressure? Or did you rise above it and keep going forward? What was God revealing to you about yourself during this time?

Stop and Jot in Your Notebook!

Takeaways:

➤ Daily challenges make you stronger.

➤ Have confidence in yourself.

➤ Act accordingly when you face trials.

Encouragement:

These life lessons are designed to help you to understand how to react when life is difficult and things don't seem to be going right. Your perspective and your reaction makes the difference. **When times are challenging, do a two-step. Dance, sing, pray, shout, cry or run. In other words, do what it takes to bring yourself back from the brink of quitting.** *Stand firm in what you believe when life comes to defeat you and deflate you.*

There Has to Be More!

As we grow into the age of accountability, we must all realize that there is more than just living life as we know it—being born, going to school, growing up, going to school some more, getting a job, getting married, having children, going through the empty nest syndrome, retiring and then dying. There has to be more. If there has to be more, then what is it and where is it? Those are the big questions, and, hopefully, we all ask them early in life rather than later, when it may be way too late.

To all of those who are at the age of knowing God and can be accountable to Him, Proverbs 22:6 says:

> *Train up a child in the way he should go: and when he is old, he will not depart from it.*

Voila! This is the key to finding *more*. The journey to find *more* begins as a child. Training for life begins when you are a child, and the way you spend your childhood sets your life into motion. It determines how difficult or how easy your path will be. Give attention to this short excerpt from Luke 2:41-52 (NKJV) entitled "The Boy Jesus Amazes the Scholars":

His parents went to Jerusalem every year at the Feast of the Passover. And when He was twelve years old, they went up to Jerusalem according to the custom of the feast. When they had finished the days, as they returned, the Boy Jesus lingered behind in Jerusalem. And Joseph and His mother did not know it; but supposing Him to have been in the company, they went a day's journey, and sought Him among their relatives and acquaintances. So when they did not find Him, they returned to Jerusalem, seeking Him. Now so it was that after three days they found Him in the temple, sitting in the midst of the teachers, both listening to them and asking them questions. And all who heard Him were astonished at His understanding and answers. So when they saw Him, they were amazed; and His mother said to Him, "Son, why have You done this to us? Look, Your father and I have sought You anxiously."
And He said to them, "Why did you seek Me? Did you not know that I must be about My Father's business?" But they did not understand the statement which He spoke to them.

Then He went down with them and came to Nazareth, and was subject to them, but His mother kept all these things in her heart. And Jesus increased in wisdom and stature, and in favor with God and men.

How truly amazing! Jesus set the example for us, showing us that children can be used by God. He also let His parents know that He had a purpose and that He was fulfilling it already at the age of twelve. In this way, Jesus was bringing to His parents the awareness that He was born of the Holy Spirit and would not live a normal or natural life. He had a supernatural purpose on this earth.

Even though Jesus' parents did not fully understand the call on His life yet, they knew that He was anointed by God. Later, the Bible states in verse 51, Jesus *"was subject"* to His parents, which meant that He honored them and obeyed them as a child should.

Then, verse 52, states that *"Jesus increased in wisdom and stature, and in favor with God and men."* That is the key.

Just as Jesus was about His father's business when He was still a child, God is still looking for parents today who will be used as teachers, to develop, train and nurture children who will serve God and understand their purpose early in life. He is searching for children who will not be void of understanding and not know God but, rather, children who will recognize who they are in

There Has to Be More!

Christ early and will walk in wisdom and have the favor of God and man.

Here is another example, this one from Jeremiah 1:4-8 (NKJV). This Bible lesson is entitled "The Call of Jeremiah":

> *Then the word of the Lord came to me, saying: "Before I formed you in the womb I knew you; before you were born I sanctified you; I ordained you a prophet to the nations."*
>
> *Then said I: "Ah, Lord God! Behold, I cannot speak, for I am a youth."*
>
> *But the Lord said to me: "Do not say, 'I am a youth,' for you shall go to all to whom I send you, and whatever I command you, you shall speak. Do not be afraid of their faces, for I am with you to deliver you," says the Lord.*

During the Old Testament years, the standard was set, that children can be used by the Lord even in their youth. God was telling Jeremiah not to make excuses for why he could not be used. He told Jeremiah that He had formed him, set him apart and appointed him when he was still in his mother's womb. If God did that with Jeremiah, that means that He also did it with you and me. We know what His Word says in Malachi 3:6:

> *For I am the LORD, I change not.*

This is good news. You were touched by God even before you left your mother's womb. This means that you are to walk in your purpose, finding out what the MORE is that God has for you.

Parents, be a vessel that God uses to train up your children and encourage them in the things of God. Teach them His statutes and His ways. Be a source of support that your children can call on when they need you the most. To do this, you need to be a few steps ahead of your children in seeking God for your own life, so that you can prepare them for their destiny. As you serve your children in this way, God will honor you, and you will also find yourself walking in the "more" of God simultaneously with your children.

Just as Mary and Joseph were used by God to usher Jesus onto the scene, every mother and father living today has the opportunity to raise up a generation of children who love Him. As a parent, I know that parenting in the twenty-first century is not easy. You will have many challenges to face, many difficult decisions to make, and a huge amount of responsibility as a caretaker of God's little ones. But the good news is this: just as God visited Mary and Joseph at the time of Mary's conception, He will visit every woman who is to give birth to a child.

Of course, there will never be another virgin birth or the birth of another savior, but the child you carry has a divine purpose, just as Jesus did. And it's just as important that you hear what the Spirit is saying, to raise that child in God's way.

There Has to Be More!

The Bible says, in Psalm 127:3:

Lo, children are an heritage of the Lord: and the fruit of the womb is his reward.

When the Father gives you a reward, it is for your delight and your pleasure. That child you were given is your heritage here on earth. Many times we neglect the relationships the Lord gives us and fail to invest the time and effort required for developing that heritage for the generations to come.

God knew what He was doing when He created families. It was never His plan that man live on this earth alone and without support. A family was designed by God to provide strength, fellowship, nurturing, peace and so much more. When you neglect the family, you are actually hindering the will of God in your life.

I remember the days of my youth very well. We spent a lot of time going to the country to visit my grandmother. There we picked blackberries and rolled up and down the hills. When we finished playing, we all walked to the corner store to buy a bag of penny candy and pickles. What a time we had! I lived for those days.

It was like living a dream. We were experiencing nature and enjoying the fruit of the ground, Mom and Dad were happy, we kids were happy and, in my opinion, it just couldn't get any better. Life was good, everybody seemed to have a place, and everybody was in their place, fulfilling the role God put them in.

What would it be like if we allowed God to freely manifest Himself through us as adults? When we grow older, things don't seem to flow nearly as smoothly as when we were younger. Sooner or later, problems arise and challenges come to distract us from our purpose. What will we do then? Can God still cause the family to be in harmony one with another? Can we find God's peace in the midst of turmoil? When the enemy comes against the family, can we stand and see the salvation of the Lord? My answer is, YES, we can absolutely see God manifest His power in our lives for good. You have to remember that God created the family. Therefore, His hand of love, guidance and protection is ever present to bring victory when challenges arise.

I learned a lot during my youth. When I think about Jesus and how His mother found Him in the temple about His father's business, it let's me know that Jesus had a passion to bring the Father's will to pass even as a boy. He didn't wait until He had become an adult to find out what God had predestined for Him. He owned His calling and began to walk in it early, and He was focused on the prize set before Him. Not only that, but Jesus had to be content for a time when other people didn't yet understand who He was. When they spoke to Him, they didn't realize that they were interacting with the Son of God. He knew His royalty and deity, and yet He humbled himself and let God use Him to His glory.

Jesus began this journey as an infant and allowed His vision and purpose to mature over many years. He didn't get anxious or tired of being a common man among the people. He didn't rush the process so that He could receive His accolades and praise and be validated as the Almighty Son of God. He allowed the Father's plan to evolve in the fullness of time.

Remember, when Jesus walked on earth, He walked as a man, and He had to overcome the same trials and temptations we face. Some may ask, "Why did Jesus have to become a man to save us?" I can assure you that it was God's plan to save man and bring him back to Himself after Adam and Eve had sinned. Isaiah 55:8-9 states:

> *For my thoughts are not your thoughts, neither are your ways my ways, saith the LORD. For as the heavens are higher than the earth, so are my ways higher than your ways, and my thoughts than your thoughts.*

In other words, God does some things because He is God, and who are we to question the mind of God? Some things may never be revealed until the fullness of time.

With all of that said, Jesus definitely knew that there was "more" to life that just good times. He had a calling to fulfill. Let Jesus the Christ be our example of seeking God's will early and not wasting time because of our age.

LIFE LESSON 2
SELF-CHECK

Our Father God created us with a divine purpose in mind from the moment of conception. Sometimes people work their entire lives trying to figure out why they were born and what their purpose in life is. Well, when you are child of God, He leads you into that purpose. Without Him, it can be like trying to find a needle in a haystack. Have you found your purpose in life?

Stop and Jot in Your Notebook!

Takeaways:

➢ The Lord orders your steps.

➢ When you pray, ask the Lord to reveal His plan and purpose for your life.

➢ When the Lord begins to speak to you through small things, pay attention!

Encouragement

The Bible says that *"faith is the substance of things hoped for, the evidence of things not seen."* It also says that *"the just shall live by faith."* It is our responsibility. as believers, to trust God. No, it won't be easy, but we cannot focus on how things look. We have to trust that God is in control. When we pray and read the Word, we will know when it's God speaking. His Word also says, *"My sheep know my voice, and a stranger they will not follow."* Be encouraged! If you see the signs of His Word and hear His voice in prayer, you will walk in His path.

Life Lesson 3

On My Way to More!

I was eighteen. I had been a successful student, making good grades, and I had favor with all my teachers. I was a "goody two-shoes" if you will. After high school, I started college and got a job working at City Hall and then the Post Office. At that time, this was a major accomplishment for a girl my age. Life was good. I was happy, and my life was all planned out.

I was determined to be a successful businesswoman. I was making money hand over fist; and nothing would be able to stop me. I starting small entrepreneurial endeavors, making and selling candy apples and popcorn balls. I also scavenged around the house for old items in good condition that could be sold at our local flea market. As I got older, I began making and selling arts and crafts, ceramics, T-shirts and other items. I was on the right track, earning an extra one to two thousand dollars a week in addition to my paycheck at the post office, and I was still a young adult. But I was working myself to death.

I was up all night getting orders ready, achieving my dream of being an entrepreneur early. But one thing was missing: I felt unfulfilled and lonely. "There has to be more to life than just making money and being successful," I thought. Growing up wasn't proving to be all that exciting, after all. I somehow knew there had to be more.

In my heart, I began to ask questions about my future and how I could feel more fulfilled in life. I kept working and going to school, earning awards and receiving special honors for things I accomplished at school and at work, but I still had that sense of loneliness. I'll never forget what happened one day. A lady in my neighborhood stopped me on the street and said, "Girl, I like the way you walk. You are so confident. You're going places." I wondered if the lady was just crazy or if she could really see something I couldn't see. Her comments to me, combined with my loneliness and lack of fulfillment, sent me on a search for more.

I continued to do well in school, but now I started having nightmares about monsters and demons. I had never had nightmares before, so I didn't know where all of that was coming from. I didn't really believe in demons and evil spirits because the Catholic church I attended didn't talk about these things. Our priest usually taught from a newspaper article or from something on the news. I remember sitting in church one day thinking, "Is this what religion is all about?"

On My Way to More!

Jesus was rarely mentioned, only Mary, His mother, and we prayed to a lot of statues and did the stations of the cross. For those who don't know, doing the stations of the cross is a Catholic ritual in which the adherents kneel and stand, kneel and stand, as they complete each "station," meaning a location where Jesus suffered something as He carried His cross toward Calvary.

We spent whole days outside in the heat saying the Rosary. It seemed like it would never end. As a young girl, I decided that if this was what serving God was all about, I didn't want any part of it.

Even though I was sure *that* life was not for me, I knew I needed something else. I couldn't put my finger on what it was, but I had the strong feeling that it had to do with God. This may have been because my grandmother prayed for me all the time and talked to me about Jesus when she visited. She used to tell me Bible stories and tell me why it was important to serve God. Grandma's talking about Jesus made me feel very good. You could tell that she really loved Him, whoever He was. She also encouraged me to be a good girl and to serve God. By the time she had finished with me, I was getting a better understanding of what it meant to know Him.

It was then that I realized I needed God to open my eyes to my sinful self. I wasn't your typical heathen. I didn't use drugs, smoke, drink, gamble or run the streets, nor any of the other things we first think of as sin. I had no problem with the normal temptations. I had no problem with outside influences trying to seduce me into succumbing to those evil vices. Oh, no. But what I *did* have was a lot of inner demons tempting me to fear everything. My many fears included a fear of the future, of God, of relationships, of new experiences and of opportunities.

I was always over-thinking everything, even the simplest of things. If I needed to take a test, I over-thought it. If I needed to write a letter, I over-thought it. My own mind and spirit were my bondage. I had so much faith in what could go wrong or what might not be acceptable that it caused me to fear almost everything. I had so many fears that I began to feel tormented.

When I was younger, my dad was a cab driver, and I would overhear him talking to Mama about the dangers of driving a cab. Fellow cab drivers were being robbed and killed for a few dollars. Dad often worked the night shift and got home quite late, and I absolutely could not sleep until he was home safe. I was up until all hours waiting to hear him come through the door, and if it got too late and he hadn't come, panic set in. I often begged him to stop driving, but he said he couldn't because we needed the money.

When we took family drives to the country, I couldn't enjoy the fun of looking out the window and counting cars, trees and animals with my brothers and sister because, before I knew it, I was on the floor behind the driver's seat praying (in the only way I knew how) for the Lord not to let us die in a car accident.

I look back now and laugh at some of the foolishness the devil told me. I can hear Mama now saying, "Girl, what are you doing? Get up off that floor. Everything will be okay." And soon I would be back playing with my brothers and sister. They all got many laughs from my behavior.

I was so emotional as a child that I earned the nickname Crybaby. My dad never called me that. He always called me Baby Girl. It was his way of saying, "Even if you cry, that's okay. You're my Baby." Until he passed away in 2015, he continued to call me Baby Girl.

Oh, what a time I used to have just trying to survive my thoughts of gloom and doom. I was convinced that nothing was ever going to go right. I was trapped in my own head, in a place of fear and torment. As I grew older, I learned to conceal these fears from others so as not to be ridiculed by them. As a result, nobody really knew what I was going through. I was functional, and I was a fighter and, by the grace of God, I was somehow able to resist many of these fears by saying the Lord's Prayer over and over again until all the agitation and anxiety ceased.

I had one friend, Marilyn, who was a believer and often told me that Jesus loved me and didn't want me to be afraid all the time. I asked her how she know that He loved me, and she said the Lord had shown her. In time, I came to realize that she was right. After I had given my life to Jesus, thoughts of fear no longer consumed me, I no longer over-thought the simplest things, my mind didn't race at night, and I was healed and delivered from the torment of the enemy.

God's Word is true when it says in Matthew 11:28:

> *Come unto me, all ye that labour and are heavy laden, and I will give you rest.*

I found this rest when I was saved as a result of Marilyn inviting me to church on Easter Sunday morning when I was eighteen. There, at her church, I accepted Jesus as my personal Savior. It had been the grace of God that kept my mind from falling to pieces and my spirit from being utterly consumed by fear. I needed a Savior and I could not save myself. That Sunday morning I cast all of my fears upon Him.

When I went to the altar and threw my hands up, it almost seemed automatic. I hadn't known that was what I was expected to do; I just did it. I cried with relief during the rest of the service, feeling as though the world had lifted off my shoulders. Now I knew that Jesus truly does save.

That night I dreamed that I was sleeping on clouds. Not too long after that, I was filled with the Holy Spirit. God truly does deliver and, most of all, He truly does hear our prayers.

As the years passed, I would occasionally feel fear again (anytime I was not immersed in prayer and the Word), but when I felt myself slipping, I would repent before God and let Him renew my mind.

Although my parents had not been churchgoers nor saved at the time, somehow they knew the basic principles of goodness and instilled morals into me that I believe led me on my path to seek God. They taught me the desire to do right, live right and be right. As a kid, I had felt the pressure of it all. How could I live right, do right and be right when I was so imperfect?

My grandmother was also a huge influence in my life when I was a child. Because of her life, I was able to see things from a spiritual perspective. She used to pray and read the Bible all the time, and I realized that's where goodness comes from. It comes from God. Between my parents and my grandmother, God set me on a course to desire Him and His ways.

All of these events led up to a journey that would usher me into many life experiences as a child of God. Through my encounter with God that Easter Sunday, I was set up to learn what it meant to be a Christian and to wait on God, hearing from Him and submitting to Him and acknowledging Jesus as Lord and Savior. It was not just a bunch of pretty words. It was a lifestyle.

In my childhood, God allowed me to go through some trials to get me to the point of recognizing that I needed Him. Now, while many young people my age were focused on shopping, partying and other things, I was in search of my destiny. I remember being called a wallflower, when I went to a school dance and didn't dance, but just sat in a corner wondering what would happen if Jesus returned right that second. I used to look at the kids around me and wonder if they were truly happy. Ultimately, I knew that many of them weren't. They were just going through the motions, doing what people thought they should be doing at their age. But, when the party was over, they, too, wanted more. When their hangover was gone, their high faded away, or their boyfriend or girlfriend dumped them, then they realized that there had to be more.

As for me, since I had already been known as a crybaby and a scaredy cat, it didn't take much for me to say yes to Jesus. I had been looking for a way out. God had used those nightmares to draw me to Himself. I had been so frightened by them that I would wake up perspiring and hyperventilating.

I remember the very last nightmare I had. Demons were chasing me, and then the heavens opened up, and a man with a bright light rescued me just when I was about to be devoured. I had that dream the night before I accepted Jesus Christ as my Lord and Savior. And, let me tell you, after that day, the day of my salvation, I was no longer a scaredy cat. God had taken that spirit of fear from me. I was now as bold and brave as a lion.

I had always been very emotional and still have the tendency to this day to shed a tear here or there. I think it's just part of my make up. Nevertheless, the Bible says, in John 8:36:

On My Way to More!

If the Son therefore shall make you free, ye shall be free indeed.

No more shackles, no more chains, no more fear, no more worry, no more doubt and no more unbelief. I was victorious, free to be who God had called me to be. I was definitely free to be me.

I was free to believe that I could do whatever my mind thought I could do. Now there was literally no stopping me. Suddenly, the nightmares were gone, and I began to dream dreams of life and victory. Now God began to give me dreams that left me with wisdom and ideas for ministry and business.

One night, for example, I dreamed that I was reaching out to kids at a facility in my community for girls and boys who had been put out of school, out of their homes and made wards of the state. Mind you, I was still eighteen and newly saved. When I woke up the next morning, I called the facility (I had only seen it in passing) and told those in charge that I'd had a dream that I was to help them with the kids and that I wanted to know when I could start volunteering. The volunteer coordinator was shocked by this, but she invited me to come speak with her. That dream turned into four years of ministry to more than four hundred children and teens. The Lord used me to start Bible studies in every group, teach art classes and other special events for the kids, even take them to concerts and local church services on buses.

When the fear that had held me bound was broken, I felt like I could conquer the world, and the kids I ministered to were so thankful that someone would come to tend to them and their needs.

As I noted earlier, when children are born, they are supposed to be a heritage and a reward. Well, these children were not feeling like a reward or a blessing. They felt all alone and cursed. God used me to bring light into the midst of their darkness. Eventually, we had almost a hundred volunteers going to minister at that facility on a regular basis. That's what the power of God can do.

Those early teen years in ministry set me on a course to always put God first in all things. I had seen many miracles at a young age, and the Lord had certainly done a lot for me already. I felt like I could relate a little to Jesus, when He told Mary that He must be about His Father's business.

It was then that I knew why God had called me, but little did I know that the Father had so much more in store for me and that this was just the tip of the iceberg. I began to grow and grow and grow some more in ministry, seeking God's will for my own life even as I ministered to hurting kids.

Of course, whenever you're walking in God's plan, the enemy will always, without fail, raise his ugly head. But God is right there to stablish you, strengthen you and make you perfect. The more you work for God, the more you need Him on a daily basis because He is the Source you draw from.

LIFE LESSON 3
SELF-CHECK

Everyone has to have an encounter with God the Father. When we're seeking, we don't always know what we're looking for, but God, in His infinite wisdom, allows life circumstances, a godly friend, a pastor or a divine incident to help us to realize that it is God we are longing for. Have you begun to wonder why you were created and what is your purpose?

Stop and Jot in Your Notebook!

When was the last time you felt that you were empty on the inside? What did you do to try to satisfy that emptiness? Did it work? What now?

Takeaways:

> **Look in the mirror!**

> **Search your heart!**

Encouragement:

The Bible says, *"The earth is the Lord's, and the fulness thereof; the world, and they that dwell therein"* (Psalm 24:1). This means you are included because you are in the earth. If you have been trying to figure out what's wrong or what's missing or asking yourself, "Why can't I get my life together?", I admonish you to TRY JESUS!

Without Him, I Can Do Nothing!

In the midst of all the great things that were happening in my life, I have to recognize that if it were not for God being on my side, I would have been consumed by my own desires. If it were not for Him, I would have lost my mind, my family and my Jesus. It is important to always stay humble, knowing that it's not you that's winning the people, but it is the Lord. You have to stay in touch with the fact that you are only a vessel for the Master's use. It's all about someone else coming to the knowledge of Christ.

In spite of all that I learned as a young lady, years later I'm still learning that I need my Savior every day of my life. Receiving Him is not a one-time event. I can't go one second without His guidance and grace because as soon as I think I have it altogether, my own the flesh and that old Slewfoot raise their ugly heads. The great apostle Paul wrote that God had sent him a *"thorn in the flesh"* to buffet him so that he would not become proud (see 2 Corinthians 12:7). The same is true today. God knows what you need to keep you on track, and He can (and will) use the enemy to provide it. Interestingly enough, this is how God allows goodness and mercy to follow you all the days of your life. He makes all things work together for your good—including all the aggravation and pestering from the nuisances of an enemy—to keep you remembering your need of a Savior. We will need Him until His return.

Psalm 51:5 teaches:

> *Behold, I was shapen in iniquity; and in sin did my mother conceive me.*

This shows that since coming into the world, we all need a Redeemer. Each of us enters this realm with our own generational curses to acknowledge and overcome in Jesus' name. The awakening of a man to his true state, when he comes of age, is an experience every soul must have in order to encounter Jesus. Every time we hear a call to repentance we have the opportunity to accept Jesus as our Lord and Savior. When He comes in, the curse of sin and death have no more dominion over us. As the Bible states in 1 Corinthians 15:55:

O death, where is thy sting? O grave, where is thy victory?

Jesus took the keys of death and Hell that we might be redeemed from the curse of sin. We were bought with a price. Therefore, every newborn baby that enters the world in sin will have the choice of redemption. Jesus' blood is available to wash and cleanse him.

Many new believers don't realize that when they start the journey to know Christ, the way will be filled with trials and temptations, and there will be both victories and defeats. The only difference is that now we have God on our side to help us through each battle. The Scriptures say in Luke 22:31-32:

> *And the Lord said, Simon, Simon, behold, Satan hath desired to have you, that he may sift you as wheat: but I have prayed for thee, that thy faith fail not: and when thou art converted, strengthen thy brethren.*

In other words, the enemy will come to tempt you in order to cause you to sin, but we have an Advocate who goes before the Father on our behalf. He is Jesus Christ, the Righteous One (see 1 John 2:1). The way won't be easy, and it won't be one battle and one wilderness. Your journey will be filled with many opportunities to call on Jesus to be glorified by enabling you to overcoming temptations and trials. He said in John 12:32:

And I, if I be lifted up from the earth, will draw all men unto me.

It is true that the Word was here making reference to Jesus' destiny to die on the cross and be resurrected, but we can also relate this to the moments when we die to self and overcome temptation. In those moments, we are also allowing Jesus to be lifted up so that everyone around us can see Him.

No matter how many accolades you have received in life, no matter how old you are when you accept Christ, no matter what your status in life or your family tree, you will go on a journey that reveals your need of a Savior. You will then realize that you cannot achieve victory on your own, but that God has a plan for you. As we know, all things work together for the good of those who love the Lord and are called according to His purpose (see Romans 8:28). As you walk your walk, things will happen that are good, and other things will happen that are bad, but in the midst of it all, God will order circumstances to work out for your good. You will discover what Paul expressed in Romans 7:14-25:

For we know that the law is spiritual: but I am carnal, sold under sin. For that which I do I allow not: for what I would, that do I not; but what I hate, that do I. If then I do that which I would not, I consent unto the law that it is good. Now then it is no more I that do it, but sin that dwelleth in me. For I know that in me (that is, in my flesh,) dwelleth no good thing: for to will is present with me; but how to perform that which is good I find not. For the good that I would I do not: but the evil which I would not, that I do. Now if I do that I would not, it is no more I that do it, but sin that dwelleth in me. I find then a law, that, when I would do good, evil is present with me.

For I delight in the law of God after the inward man: but I see another law in my members, warring against the law of my mind, and bringing me into captivity to the law of sin which is in my members. O wretched man that I am! who shall deliver me from the body of this death? I thank God through Jesus Christ our Lord. So then with the mind I myself serve the law of God; but with the flesh the law of sin.

Wow! Paul realized that no matter how dedicated he was to God, sin was always present, and there was an ever-present conflict in his body and spirit. In essence, he was saying that because of the law of sin and death, he would always have to struggle to put and keep his flesh under subjection. He would always need Jesus Christ as his personal Lord and Savior to help him win the victory in his daily walk.

Without Him, I Can Do Nothing!

Even though we have need of a Savior, however, the Lord did not intend for us to punish ourselves because of shortcomings and sins. When our heart is to do God's will and to serve Him, He knows that. What is important is that we not *practice* sin. *"What shall we say then? Shall we continue in sin, that grace may abound? God forbid. How shall we, that are dead to sin, live any longer therein?"* (Romans 6:1-2).

When we have trials in the flesh and are tossed to and fro between sin and righteousness, the Lord has made provision for that as well, as we see in Romans 8:1-4:

> *Where is therefore now no condemnation to them which are in Christ Jesus, who walk not after the flesh, but after the Spirit. For the law of the Spirit of life in Christ Jesus hath made me free from the law of sin and death. For what the law could not do, in that it was weak through the flesh, God sending his own Son in the likeness of sinful flesh, and for sin, condemned sin in the flesh: that the righteousness of the law might be fulfilled in us, who walk not after the flesh, but after the Spirit.*

When you desire to walk after the Spirit, Jesus Christ the Righteous will strengthen you to walk in the Spirit and not in the flesh. You will find it easier to overcome the things that used to bind you and cause you to fall. Submission to God's will produces the ability to do the right thing and resist the devil so that he will flee from you.

When and if you do sin, you know that it is not God's will for you to condemn yourself, but, instead, to go boldly before the throne of grace to find help in the time of need. It's like conditioning yourself for a marathon. When you sign up for that marathon, you know some of your routines and eating habits have to change if your mind and body are to be ready for the race. Therefore, you pay careful attention to what you're taking into your body and whether or not you are getting the proper exercise and everything else that goes along with getting ready for victory.

It's the same in the race we run as believers. We must condition our body, mind and spirit to be overcomers through prayer, fasting, reading the Word and speaking the Word, realizing that we only win with Jesus. And, you must be in this for the long haul. No one enters a race, just to quit in the middle or even before it starts.

There are several scriptures that make reference to the fact that the Christian life is a race:

2 Timothy 4:7
> *I have fought a good fight, I have finished my course,*
> *I have kept the faith.*

Hebrews 12:1 (NKJV)
> *Therefore, since we have so great a cloud of witnesses surrounding us, let us also lay aside every encumbrance and the sin which so easily entangles*

us, and let us run with endurance the race that is set before us,

1 Corinthians 9:24-27

Know ye not that they which run in a race run all, but one receiveth the prize? So run, that ye may obtain. And every man that striveth for the mastery is temperate in all things. Now they do it to obtain a corruptible crown; but we an incorruptible. I therefore so run, not as uncertainly; so fight I, not as one that beateth the air: but I keep under my body, and bring it into subjection: lest that by any means, when I have preached to others, I myself should be a castaway.

Galatians 5:7

Ye did run well; who did hinder you that ye should not obey the truth?

Philippians 2:16

Holding forth the word of life; that I may rejoice in the day of Christ, that I have not run in vain, neither laboured in vain.

Philippians 3:14

I press toward the mark for the prize of the high calling of God in Christ Jesus.

I listed all of these scriptures because in order to win the race, you must first realize that you are in one. This Christian walk has all the elements of a physical race except that it is spiritual. In this race, you will face challenges and hardships, but you can endure them as a good soldier, knowing that your training, your equipping, your pacing, your running the race, falling down and getting up again are all crucial elements to you getting to the end and the prize that awaits. So, pace yourself for this race. Thankfully, God's Word promises, in Matthew 10:22:

But he who endures to the end will be saved.

But just as we can desire the things of God, we can also desire the things of the flesh and, according to the Bible, in the flesh *"dwelleth no good thing"* (Romans 7:18). In the very next chapter of Romans, after Paul talks about overcoming his flesh and the frustrations and struggles with sin when you have a heart to do right, he talks about the end result of following after the flesh. Take note of Romans 8:5-14:

For they that are after the flesh do mind the things of the flesh; but they that are after the Spirit the things of the Spirit. For to be carnally minded is death; but to be spiritually minded is life and peace. Because the carnal mind is enmity against God: for it is not subject to the law of God, neither indeed can be. So then they that are in the flesh cannot please God.

Without Him, I Can Do Nothing!

But ye are not in the flesh, but in the Spirit, if so be that the Spirit of God dwell in you. Now if any man have not the Spirit of Christ, he is none of his. And if Christ be in you, the body is dead because of sin; but the Spirit is life because of righteousness. But if the Spirit of him that raised up Jesus from the dead dwell in you, he that raised up Christ from the dead shall also quicken your mortal bodies by his Spirit that dwelleth in you.

Therefore, brethren, we are debtors, not to the flesh, to live after the flesh. For if ye live after the flesh, ye shall die: but if ye through the Spirit do mortify the deeds of the body, ye shall live. For as many as are led by the Spirit of God, they are the sons of God.

In order for you to be a son of God, you have to be led by the Spirit of God. If you are not led by the Spirit, then you cannot rightfully call yourself a son. Let me say it another way: if you won't allow God to lead you, you cannot be His son. We have to be willing to surrender our life—our everything—to the Father. When that happens, you will immediately begin to see a manifestation of the presence of God in your life like you have never seen before.

LIFE LESSON 4
SELF-CHECK

Are you listening to what's going on in your life? Where are you lacking? When you finally submit to God's pulling on your spirit, that's when you will begin to understand that all of the circumstances and situations in your life are divinely leading you to Jesus. The Bible says, in Romans 8:28, *"And we know that all things work together for good to them that love God, to them who are the called according to his purpose."*

Stop and Jot in Your Notebook!

Takeaways:

> Everyone goes through something that leads them to the opportunity to meet and accept Christ.

> Whether you accept that opportunity or not, it will be presented to you!

> If you want to achieve more in life, accept Christ!

Encouragement:

Everyone has a story. No one is exempt from trials or tribulations. Though these may be different for every one of us, you are guaranteed to experience some challenges on your way to the cross. The good thing is that your story can have a happy and godly ending, if you will look past your issues to Christ, who is beckoning for you. Salvation is the key to more. Matthew 6:33 says: *"But seek first the kingdom of God and His righteousness, and all these things shall be added to you."*

Life Lesson # 5

A New Day

When we were little, Mama would wake us up and get us dressed to go to church; my sister and I in all those beautiful dresses and shoes Mom had purchased for us, and our brothers were dressed to the nines as well. Our hair was perfect, and everything matched. Mama always prepared us to look great, not just for church, but for any occasion. Every new day brought a new appreciation to the phrase: "Be your best."

That reminds me of what Jesus said in John 14:2-3:

> *I go to prepare a place for you. And if I go and prepare a place for you, I will come again, and receive you unto myself; that where I am, there ye may be also.*

God wants us to look good. He wants the best for us, so much so that He actually prepared a place for us. His Word says that He wishes above all things that we prosper and be in health even as our soul prospers (see 3 John 1:2). He wants to restore what we have lost and replace our mourning with gladness. He said in His Word that He will restore the years that the locusts and the cankerworm have eaten (see Joel 2:25). He desires to give us new beginnings to old promises.

Our heavenly Father is a God who prepares us for special occasions, so that we look our best and are always ready for anything that might present itself. He says in His Word, in Jeremiah 29:11:

> *For I know the thoughts that I think toward you, saith the Lord, thoughts of peace, and not of evil, to give you an expected end.*

God promises in Lamentations 3:23:

> *They [the Lord's mercies] are new every morning.*

This means that you have new mercy every day, new opportunities to do it better. Wow! Double Wow! NEW MERCIES EVERY MORNING!

Have you ever felt like you had used up all of your allotment of mercy? Well, God made a provision for the moments when you are weary and worn, and it can't get any better than that! We have no reason to fail. That's the kind of God we serve. He sets us up for success, victory, dominion and all those other words that symbolize king-ship. After you have experienced your day of salvation, you get to realize many more new beginnings to old promises being fulfilled. God is never slack concerning His promises (see 2 Peter 3:9), and His promises are *"yea"* and *"amen"* (2 Corinthians 1:20).

God has also said that we can *"come boldly unto the throne of grace, that we may obtain mercy, and find grace to help in time of need"* (Hebrews 4:16). Another Wow! Double Wow! I can go to God's throne to get the grace I need.

What is grace? It is God's unmerited favor. UNMERIT-ED, UNEARNED, UNDESERVED, UNWARRANTED favor coming on me? God must really love me! He has put me into position to live the God kind of life, a life of true happiness.

The revelation that I can go before the throne of God to get help in the time of my need floored me. It changed my whole way of thinking. It was then that I knew I could access God in real time, meaning that no matter what was going on or when it was going on, I could pray, and God would hear me. This phenomenal concept set me free from the thought of being on my own. I could really touch God, making contact with the heavenly Father. So, whatever He was calling me for, I knew that He would equip me for His purpose.

With that revelation in mind, God began training and equipping me to thrive in this world as a child of God. He is reaching back to you, as you reach up to Him, making the divine connection that you could not find in the wilderness because it is a place of consecration. That is God breaking through the bondages and spiritual wickedness to deliver you, God giving you the oil of gladness for the spirit of heaviness, God Himself taking off your current cloak of sackcloth and ashes, to replace it with a coat of many colors, God being magnified in you in the earth.

God is equipping you for the work of the ministry. Whether you are called to the five-fold ministry or you are a lay person in the church, we are all conduits for Christ. So, we must stay in constant communication with the Father. It is imperative that we maintain a life of prayer, fasting and studying the Word of God. That will ensure that you can hear God, even when He speaks in a whisper, because your spirit man is listening.

This divine connection is made only after you have decided to say "yes" and be obedient to God's Word. Then He can give you the needed tools (wisdom, knowledge and understanding) to overcome life's obstacles because you are in a place to hear. Before, you were blinded by the cares of this life and could not receive the things of God because they were foolishness to you.

As you make this divine connection with God, He is removing the spirit of bondage. He is giving you the oil of gladness for the spirit of heaviness. He is taking away the cloak of sackcloth and ashes and replacing it with the coat of many colors.

A New Day

His favor is upon you to do exceedingly, abundantly more than you can ask or think. The Scriptures declare, in Luke 4:18-19:

> *The Spirit of the Lord is upon me, because he hath anointed me to preach the gospel to the poor; he hath sent me to heal the brokenhearted, to preach deliverance to the captives, and recovering of sight to the blind, to set at liberty them that are bruised, to preach the acceptable year of the Lord.*

God is all over you. Rejoice and be glad. The wilderness season defines who you are and sets God's approval upon you to do wondrous works.

LIFE LESSON 5
<u>SELF-CHECK</u>

Did you know that the Lord has provided everything you need to walk in victory? Many times we take the grace of God for granted. We constantly pray for things to happen when we are not using the tools God has already given us to access those things. Are you overlooking what the Father has given you to be successful? Are you praying daily? Are you reading your Bible? Are you speaking the Word of God over your life and family?

<u>Stop and Jot in Your Notebook!</u>

<u>Takeaways:</u>

> ➤ Practice praying and reading the Word of God on a daily basis!

> ➤ Trust that God will answer when your prayers are aligned with His Word.

<u>Encouragement:</u>

You are not alone! You are an heir of Christ. Know who you are in Christ by reading the Word of God and declaring the promises of God over your life.

Stop the Insanity

As you listen to the Holy Spirit, He will reveal to you what is needed. You have to let go of old offences, old wounds, old hurts. You have to come out of the past and focus on the future. He will shine the light on the condition of your heart. Do as Paul did, as recorded in Philippians 3:13-14:

> *Forgetting those things which are behind, and reaching forth unto those things which are before, I press toward the mark for the prize of the high calling of God in Christ Jesus.*

When you trust God, you will reap where you have not sown. Build up *"the old waste places"* (Isaiah 58:12) and equip yourself for the coming outpouring. Remove the stain of loss from your life (see Romans 6:14), and proclaim newness of life. Then, let your light shine before men (see Matthew 5:16) and be steadfast and unmovable (see 1 Corinthians 15:58).

A crucial part of coming out of the wilderness is forgiving others. You must take on the very nature of God, when it comes to letting go of the past. You have to believe that just as He cast your sins into the sea of forgetfulness and removed them as far as the east is from the west (see Psalm 103:12), you can forgive yourself and others in like manner. You can accomplish this by *"Looking unto Jesus the author and finisher of our faith"* (Hebrews 12:2). Refuse to be entangled again with the yoke of bondage (see Galatians 5:1), knowing that he who the Son has set free is free indeed (see John 8:36).

Have you heard the old saying, "When it rains, it pours"? For a time, it seemed as though that was my life story. And, when there was trouble on every side, it was easy to blame myself for everything that had gone wrong and was going wrong.

Then, in the midst of this whirlwind, my marriage began falling apart due to the demands and pressures of ministry, work and family. As a result, I felt like I had disappointed God and my children. The truth is that if we had the opportunity to do it differently, we would probably spend more time seeking God's face for the marriage. After twenty years of marriage, it was over. Unfortunately, we sometimes take things for granted.

"Why and how did that happen?" At that point, it was a rhetorical question. I knew we should have focused more on the marriage. I considered myself holy and a good steward of the things of God, especially of my own household. Now God showed me that I had no reason to linger in unforgiveness, bitterness, rejection, depression or any other state of mind that was contrary to His will. I needed to give it all to Him and move on.

The Holy Spirit's light will allow you see what's in the corners and crevices of your heart. Is it of God? Or is it of the flesh? Is it a hinderance to your spiritual growth?

Still, my marriage was not easy to let go of. After all, I had invested twenty whole years of my life into it. Afterward I spent several years in this area of the wilderness because I just could not stop asking *how* and *why* until finally God showed me that if I chose to remain in that state of defeat, I would ultimately surrender my purpose to the enemy. I would only draw on things that agreed with my mind.

Then I decided to give it all to Jesus, stop asking *why* and *how* and just realize that divorce was now a part of my story. It was then that I began to accept God's promises for my life and move on.

No more crying over spilled milk, I picked up the broken pieces of my life and started all over again. Forward! Onward and upward! I refused to be entangled again with the yoke of bondage and knew that in God I was free indeed. I determined to wait on the Lord, knowing His promises in 1 Peter 5:10:

But the God of all grace, who hath called us unto his eternal glory by Christ Jesus, after that ye have suffered a while, make you perfect, stablish, strengthen, settle you.

Once I began to stand on the promises again (despite the fact that I was getting divorced), I began to see the light of day. No more dwelling on what went wrong, now I focused on knowing that I was the righteousness of God in Christ Jesus (see 2 Corinthians 5:21), that old things were passing away and all things were becoming new (see 2 Corinthians 5:17), that I was more than a conqueror in Christ Jesus (see Romans 8:37).

Life had to go on, even when things had not gone the way I expected. God still loved me, and He still had me in the palm of his hand. It was in Him that I lived and moved and had my being (see Acts 17:28). I refused to allow my own negative thoughts of defeat and rejection to have dominion over my spirit. I would NOT be entangled again with the yoke of bondage. I was free in God, and I would wait upon Him to strengthen me, stablish me and make me perfect.

Attempting to restart my life, I had to regularly rehearse the promises of God. This built me up. I spent a lot of time encouraging myself in the Lord. With each passing day, I had to remember that I was the righteousness of God in Christ Jesus. The more I spoke the Word over my life, the more I could see God restoring me and opening new doors for me to walk through.

Stop the Insanity

Trust me, this didn't happen overnight. Being around certain people, certain things or certain environments would set me back and cause me to remember things that had offended me or made me angry. Each and every time, I had to speak to myself and force myself to snap out of it and bounce back from those thoughts.

I kept rehearsing the truths of the Scriptures, that old things had passed away and all things had become new. I said it over and over to myself until I had gained authority over the thoughts from the past that were trying to invade my mind. More than anything, I had to be responsible and maintain the victory that God had given me, not only for myself, but also for my children's sake. They were counting on me to be more than a survivor. I needed to be an overcomer.

In time I was able to take the lemons life offered me and make lemonade. There was no turning back. Therefore, I had to move forward. I had to get a grip on my circumstances, not only for myself, but also for the sake of my children. I was *not* going to die in that wilderness of shame, defeat, regret and all the other negative adjectives that described my life at the time. I was going to show everyone around me what I was made of—the image of God.

I knew the truth of Proverbs 24:16 well:

For a just man falleth seven times, and riseth up again.

Truthfully, it was not about me showing someone else what I was made of; it was all about me showing myself that I could overcome any hurdle (including this one) and that I would be better than ever when it was all over.

You are the maestro of your own orchestra, and your orchestra will play when you raise the baton. The musicians will let the music flow, as you move the baton back and forth to the left and to the right. The intensity of the music will increase with every thrust of the baton. And, finally, when you lower the baton to stop the music, the orchestra will indeed stop, and you will receive your standing ovation.

In other words, you are in control, and people respect your talent and ability to direct and manage your own life. You march to your own beat. Don't let anyone dictate your music. Don't let anyone stop your flow by infringing their lifestyle or their sin upon you. Stand up and break the cycle of sin in your life. Lay aside those weights, even if they are best friends, family members, co-workers or fellow church members. You have a calling to fulfill, so press toward the mark of the prize of the high calling in Christ Jesus (see Philippians 3:14).

Walk as though you are a king or a queen. You ought to live as though any goal is reachable. In other words, you ought to live like you have dominion because you do.

Be careful not to spend time ministering to others while losing who you are and what your purpose in life is.

Stop the Insanity

As you are coming out of the wilderness, you need to resist those things, those people and those situations that try to drag you back to a place of defeat, depression and disconnection from the things of God. Just as Jesus gave us an example of how we *should* go through the wilderness, the Israelites gave us an example of how *not* to go through the wilderness.

Wake up and smell the coffee. There was a famous weight-loss guru some years ago who often said, "Stop the insanity." When you continue to do the same things over and over again and you get the same unwanted results, that's insanity. God's Word tells us:

Hebrews 12:1-2

Wherefore seeing we also are compassed about with so great a cloud of witnesses, let us lay aside every weight, and the sin which doth so easily beset us, and let us run with patience the race that is set before us, looking unto Jesus the author and finisher of our faith; who for the joy that was set before him endured the cross, despising the shame, and is set down at the right hand of the throne of God.

Galatians 5:1

Stand fast therefore in the liberty wherewith Christ hath made us free, and be not entangled again with the yoke of bondage.

John 8:36

> *If the Son therefore shall make you free, ye shall be free indeed.*

Galatians 5:16-17

> *This I say then, Walk in the Spirit, and ye shall not fulfil the lust of the flesh. For the flesh lusteth against the Spirit, and the Spirit against the flesh: and these are contrary the one to the other: so that ye cannot do the things that ye would.*

WHAT MORE CAN I SAY? It's up to you to make a conscious decision within yourself to call on the power and strength of God to make a change and STOP THE INSANITY once and for all.

LIFE LESSON 6
SELF-CHECK

Don't let life's circumstance beat you up. When things don't go the way you expected, shed your tears, wipe your face and snap out of it. Your trials make you stronger. Seasons change. You cannot become stagnant because of the appearance of failure. Sometimes you may think it's failure, but it's actually God moving you toward your destiny. You are the righteousness of God in Christ Jesus.

Stop and Jot in Your Notebook!

Are you condemning yourself for something you felt went wrong? Are you have trouble letting go of the past?

Takeaways:

> **When you walk with God, it's all in the plan!**

> **Whether you like it or not, it happened. Get over it!**

Encouragement:

Romans 8:28: *"And we know that all things work together for good to them that love God, to them who are the called according to his purpose."* Keep this scripture in your heart so that when you begin to have regrets, you can remind yourself that you are walking in God's diving purpose, and everything you go through is working together for your good.

Know Who You Are

Hebrews 12:1-2 was my scriptural foundation. It enabled me to make it through the hurdles I was facing:

> Wherefore seeing we also are compassed about with so great a cloud of witnesses, let us lay aside every weight, and the sin which doth so easily beset us, and let us run with patience the race that is set before us, looking unto Jesus the author and finisher of our faith; who for the joy that was set before him endured the cross, despising the shame, and is set down at the right hand of the throne of God.

Give other people to Jesus and don't let their actions steal your joy or interrupt your peace. Keep yourself in the place of joy. Don't try to be the fixer; let go and let God do it.

Know Who You Are

Because I now know who I am, I am coming out of the wilderness. I don't have time to entertain the things in life that only come to hinder me and get me off balance. I have learned to lay aside every weight and sin that so easily besets me. I have learned to choose my battles and not allow anyone to take my joy or lure me into situations or conversations that I don't want to be involved with. Now I am in control of my spirt man, and I won't give my peace to anyone. My joy, my peace and my contentment belong to me.

I used my God-given weapons for the battle. His Word declares in 2 Corinthians 10:4:

> *For the weapons of our warfare are not carnal, but mighty through God to the pulling down of strong holds.*

In other words, I'm in a constant battle, because I'm *in* this world but not *of* this world (see John 17:14). Therefore, the battle is not with flesh. The Bible says emphatically that the battle is not ours but the Lord's (see 2 Chronicles 20:15). With that in mind, I first gave my battle to Jesus and then walked it out in His strength. I am not the Captain of the Hosts, merely a soldier in His army.

I march to the beat of a different drummer. The cadence that I march to is one of kingship, reigning in the things of God. I have learned to clothe myself in the whole armor of God so that I may be guarded from the wiles of the enemy :

Ephesians 6:11-12

> *Put on the whole armour of God, that ye may be able to stand against the wiles of the devil. For we wrestle not against flesh and blood, but against principalities, against powers, against the rulers of the darkness of this world, against spiritual wickedness in high places.*

I know that I cannot allow myself to focus on the actions of others and become bound, but I must always realize that I'm in a spiritual battle and keep looking unto Jesus.

Look unto Jesus, child of God. We are admonished in the Scriptures to look to the hills *"from whence cometh my help. My help cometh from the Lord"* (Psalm 121:1-2). You must stop looking at the situation and look to Jesus. When you focus your sights on heavenly things, you will not be disappointed.

Learn to be smart enough to stop and pay attention to what your life is saying to you. When your life speaks to you, listen closely to see what God is saying in the midst of it all. Even when it looks like total darkness all around you, when everything is going wrong, failure is on every hand, friends are not there like they used to be, and family is focusing on the wrong things, know this one thing: It may look dark all around, but the reality is that all you have to do is call on God and surrender to Him and He, as God Almighty, El Shaddai, will click the light on so that you might see Him, the omnipresent One there in your darkness. When you think you are alone and there is no way out, God will show up. When you are at the end of your rope and have counted yourself out, God will manifest Himself out of nowhere and come to your rescue.

As you're learning how to be successful coming out of the wilderness, you'll want to pay careful attention to what God is saying, and you have to take one baby step at a time into your destiny, trusting that God will order your steps and direct your paths. The miracles won't happen all at once; they may happen piecemeal. God the Father will give you enough to keep you strengthened and encouraged. Too much too fast might prove detrimental.

I had a dream that my car broke down in the middle of the night in a grocery store parking lot. There were no lights, no people around, no sound, no movement—no nothing. It was totally dark, and I was totally alone. As I thought on this situation, fear began to consume me. Then I began to pray: "Lord, in the name of Jesus, show me the way. Lord, lift the darkness and help me to get out of here." After I had prayed for a while, I began to feel myself giving up. I was beginning to believe that God was not coming to rescue me.

Then, just as I prayed my last prayer, the Lord showed me the way out. Suddenly I could see one light off in the distance, and then another light came on and then another. I fell to my knees and began to thank Him for hearing my cry.

The truth is that He had heard me from the very beginning. The Word says, in Psalm 8:4:

> *What is man that thou art mindful of him? and the son of man that thou visitest him? For thou has made him a little lower than the angels.*

The Word also says that Jesus sits on the right hand of the Father (see Romans 8:34)and that He prays for you that your faith will not fail (see Luke 22:32). Daniel 10:12 shows us that God heard Daniel's prayer on the first day he prayed it.

God showed me, through that dream, that the just shall live by faith (see Romans 1:17) and not by sight (see 2 Corinthians 5:7). No matter what it looks like, no matter how long it takes, trust and wait on God to answer and deliver.

It was grace that brought me this far, and it is grace that will lead me on. It was mercy that sustained me and kept me when my soul earned judgement. It was goodness and mercy that followed me and continue to follow me. If it would not have been for the Lord who was on my side, where would I be? By Him, I have run through a troop and leaped over a wall.

It was the covenant-keeping God who drew me out with a gentle hand. It was the miraculous blood of Jesus that anchored my soul in God. It was the Spirit of God that ministered peace and direction to my soul. He gave me the

Know Who You Are

oil of gladness for the spirit of heaviness. It was God Himself who took off the cloak of sackcloth and ashes to replace it with a coat of many colors.

And it is God being magnified in you in the earth, so never say you are unworthy. No man is worthy, except through Christ, but God desires to use you for His glory.

LIFE LESSON 7 SELF-CHECK

2 Corinthian 5:17 states, "*Therefore if any man be in Christ, he is a new creature: old things are passed away; behold, all things are become new.*" This means that when you accept Christ, not only do you become a new creature, but you agree with God that you are a new creature. In essence, you must also agree to leave all of the old things that bind you behind. Your mind must be focused on going forward in His will for your life.

Stop and Jot in Your Notebook!

What are your life circumstances saying to you? Are you letting go of things that are not conducive to your success in life? Are you spending too much time on relationships that drain you and stress you out?

Takeaways:

➤ Make this your motto: #Forward Motion!

➤ You do not have time to waste time!

➤ Work while it is day, for when night comes, no man can work (see John 9:4)!

Encouragement:

You have the chance of a lifetime to make your life what you desire it to be according to God's will. Go for it! Set priorities, make some changes, and GO FORWARD!

Life Lesson #8

Coming Out of the Wilderness in Dominion and Power

Give God the glory when He manifests His goodness and kindness to you. Realize that His goodness and mercy are actually following you, as He promised in His Word (see Psalm 23:6).

Before Jesus went into the wilderness, God had placed His stamp of approval upon Him when He said, *"This is my beloved Son, in whom I am well pleased"* (Matthew 3:17). When God allows you to go into a wilderness time, He has seen and acknowledged that in you is the desire to serve Him and to fulfill His purpose in your life. Causing you to pass through the wilderness does not represent a rebuke or a judgement on God's part; rather it is His hand of acceptance and acknowledgment that you are His own.

The wilderness is not for Gods' benefit, but for yours. After having gone through your wilderness season, you will realize that you can do all things through Christ who strengthens you (see Philippians 4:13), even resisting the temptations of the enemy and coming forth as pure gold. It is a place where you hide God's Word in your heart that you might not sin against Him (see Psalm 119:11). Use that Word as Jesus did when He spoke it to Satan

Matthew 4:4

> *It is written, Man shall not live by bread alone, but every word that proceedeth out of the mouth of God.*

Matthew 4:7

> *It is written again, Thou shalt not tempt the Lord thy God.*

The enemy was persistent, but Jesus knew that He was of the Father. Again He rebuked the evil one, using the Word:

Matthew 4:10

> *Get thee hence, Satan: for It is written, Thou shalt worship the Lord thy God, and him only shalt thou serve.*

At that moment, Jesus received a spiritual manifestation of victory over Satan's greatest weapons:

- The lust of the flesh,
- The lust of the eyes, and
- The pride of life.

Jesus defeated Satan right there in the wilderness before He went to the cross. The Bible says in Matthew 4:11:

> *Then the devil leaveth him, and, behold, angles came and ministered to him.*

God will minister to you in the wilderness when you stand on His Word against the enemy.

Then, right after Jesus came out of the wilderness, He went into ministry:

Matthew 4:17

> *From that time Jesus began to preach, and to say, Repent: for the Kingdom of God is at hand.*

This is your day of destiny as well; when coming out of the wilderness, know when you have been touched by God. Know who you are in Him. Know the power that dwells in you. Jesus said that you would do greater works (see John 14:12). This became possible because of the coming of the Holy Spirit into the world:

John 16:7

> *Nevertheless I tell you the truth; It is expedient for you that I go away: for if I go not away, the Comforter will not come unto you; but if I depart, I will send him unto you.*

I can imagine that back then, when Jesus walked the earth, His disciples and the other people who loved Him didn't want Him to leave. They didn't want to lose sight of Him on earth. After all, He had performed many miracles and taught them many wonderful lessons to help them see Him as their Lord and Savior. He had walked in an authority that they had never seen before, and they loved Him and worshiped Him. They now saw Him for who He really was, God manifested in the flesh.

But Jesus had to leave them so that He could further reveal God's plan. That plan was not just to save us and redeem us to Himself, but He desired to give us total and complete victory—redemption, sanctification and justification. Then, after all of that was freely bestowed upon us, His plan was that we walk in victory here while He prepared a place for us to rule and reign forever.

Now that Jesus had gone back to the Father, God sent His Holy Spirit, the Comforter, to help us to live right here on earth. The Holy Spirit would now be our Guide, our strength, our peace—our everything—and Jesus would make intercession for us at the right hand of the Father. As we have noted, He shows us in the Word that He is praying for us that our faith does not fail.

Jesus promised His followers:

Acts 1:8

> *But ye shall receive power, after that the Holy Ghost is come upon you: and ye shall be witnesses unto me both in Jerusalem, and in all Judaea, and in Samaria, and unto the uttermost part of the earth.*

In other words, not only are we to have power to live and be victorious, but we will also have the power to be a witness of Christ working and moving in our lives. How awesome! God equips us with what we need, as His people.

When you are walking in the power of God, you must be sensitive to the Holy Spirit because He speaks to you to guide you and show you God's path. His still, small voice ushers you into God's purpose for your life. Don't take the power of the Holy Spirit for granted. He is precious, and He is God. The Bible says that the Holy Spirit will *"guide you into all truth"* (John 16:13).

LIFE LESSON 8
<u>SELF-CHECK</u>

The Bible states, in Hebrews 12:2, *"Looking unto Jesus the author and finisher of our faith; who for the joy that was set before him endured the cross, despising the shame, and is set down at the right hand of the throne of God."* Jesus paid the ultimate sacrifice so that we might have eternal life.

<u>Stop and Jot in You Notebook!</u>

<u>Takeaways</u>

> ➤ God is with you from beginning to end, for He is the Alpha and the Omega!

> ➤ Every man has been given a measure of faith!

> ➤ You have what you need!

<u>Encouragement:</u>

Philippians 1:6, *"Being confident of this very thing, that he who hath begun a good work in you will perform it until the day of Jesus Christ."* God will honor His Word. He created you, and He will walk with you as you walk with Him until the end of time. God has a good work for you to do. If you obey and follow Him, He is faithful to His promises.

Life Lesson #9

Shine the Light

Let your light so shine among men that they may see your good works and glorify your father which is in heaven. Matthew 5:16

SMILE! The light in your heart will glisten on your countenance, and men will be drawn to you. Jesus said, *"And I, if I be lifted up, will draw all men unto me"* (John 12:32).

You are the catalyst that sets off the movement of the Holy Spirit in your community, state, region or country. The shining of your light on Jesus and His marvelous works is what makes change happen.

When you tell of all the good things God has done for you and live a life that is pleasing in God's sight, others will take notice. Your life is the spark that will ignite the fire in other people. When you shine, you illuminate others, and they want to see how they can acquire that same light.

Matthew 5:13-16

> *Ye are the salt of the earth: but if the salt have lost his savour, wherewith shall it be salted? it is thenceforth good for nothing, but to be cast out, and to be trodden under foot of men. Ye are the light of the world. A city that is set on an hill cannot be hid. Neither do men light a candle, and put it under a bushel, but on a candlestick; and it giveth light unto all that are in the house. Let your light so shine before men, that they may see your good works, and glorify your Father which is in heaven.*

As the Bride of Christ, this is our responsibility. We have the duty of shining our light so that others can experience our precious Savior. We have a job to do on the earth, just as Jesus did when He was here in the flesh. His light shined so bright that it was blinding, so much so that the people who thought they were righteous became angry because they had never seen a man like Jesus. All of their theology and religion could not compare to the power and authority Jesus walked in and to His ability to get people to follow Him willingly.

When your light is shining, you will draw many, but you will also make some angry. Don't worry. God's got your back when you work in His vineyard. We have His promise:

Shine the Light

Isaiah 54:17

No weapon that is formed against thee shall prosper; and every tongue that shall rise against thee in judgment thou shalt condemn. This is the heritage of the servants of the Lord, and their righteousness is of me, saith the Lord.

You just do the work God has called you to, and He will protect and watch over you. Jesus said:

Matthew 6:33

But seek ye first the kingdom of God, and his righteousness; and all these things shall be added unto you.

In other words, if you put God and His Kingdom first, everything that you desire will be added to your life. The best part is this: The journey of getting saved, going through trials, tribulations and wilderness experiences and everything else the devil might throw at you doesn't have to be for nought. In the end, you can receive the promise of God. He said:

Jeremiah 29:11-13

I know the thoughts that I think toward you, saith the LORD, thoughts of peace, and not of evil, to give you an expected end. Then shall ye call upon me, and

*ye shall go and pray unto me, and I will hearken
unto you. And ye shall seek me, and find me, when
ye shall search for me with all your heart.*

Once again, God is saying to us, "I've got your back!
I have a plan for your success! I've made a way out of no
way! Trust Me, and I'll will deliver you and provide your
every need!"

Do you realize that when you let your light shine before men, your Father which in Heaven sees it and will
reward you? God is faithful to His Word. He who started
something good in you is faithful to complete it. The Lord
would not have saved you to leave you alone.

When Jesus had fulfilled His mission on earth, He began
to prepare His followers for His departure by letting them
know that He was not yet finished with all that He had in
store for them. He reassured them by saying:

John 14:1-4

*Let not your heart be troubled: ye believe in God,
believe also in me. In my Father's house are many
mansions: if it were not so, I would have told you.
I go to prepare a place for you. And if I go and
prepare a place for you, I will come again, and
receive you unto myself; that where I am, there ye
may be also. And whither I go ye know, and the
way ye know.*

In other words, Jesus was saying that because He had fulfilled His earthly calling, now He had to go and fulfill His heavenly calling. He had to go and get the house ready for our arrival. Then He said that He would come again and receive us back to Himself as the Bride of Christ. What an awesome Savior!

Jesus was and is the total package—perfect God and perfect man at the same time. How can we fail with a Savior like Jesus Christ? The Lord carefully orchestrated our success on this earth. Always remember: we were created in the image of God.

A well-known prosperity preacher once said, "You can't lose with the stuff I use." I'm sure that if you will think about that for a minute, you will realize what I'm trying to say. Child of God, you cannot lose with Him. For every mountain, hurdle and obstacle that you face, God has already given you the victory.

Psalm 18:29-36

> *For by thee I have run through a troop; and by my God have I leaped over a wall. As for God, his way is perfect: the word of the LORD is tried: he is a buckler to all those that trust in him. For who is God save the LORD? or who is a rock save our God? It is God that girdeth me with strength, and maketh my way perfect. He maketh my feet like hinds' feet, and setteth me upon my high places. He teacheth*

my hands to war, so that a bow of steel is broken by mine arms.
Thou hast also given me the shield of thy salvation: and thy right hand hath holden me up, and thy gentleness hath made me great. Thou hast enlarged my steps under me, that my feet did not slip.

Wow! Did you read that? This means that you are equipped for WHATEVER comes your way, and I mean WHATEVER! Sometimes, depending on the trial, we have to dig down deep to find the power of God to overcome. But it is there, child of God. It is there! You have been given the power to overcome evil. The Lord is the Captain of the Hosts, and He knows how to prepare you for every battle.

LIFE LESSON 9
SELF-CHECK

Your life should be like a ray of sunshine to those who are watching. Even though we all go through trials, the people around us should still be able to see that something is extra special about how we handle the toughest situations. When we learn to go through life's hardships with an inward "knowing" of victory because of our relationship with Christ, it is then that we can truly have a countenance that exudes confidence, peace and victory.

Stop and Jot in Your Notebook!

Is your light shining, or are you smiling on the inside and no one sees it? What adjustments can you make in your daily walk to ensure that your light is shining in order to draw others to Christ?

Takeaways:

➢ Illuminate the world you live in!

➢ Beam on purpose!

Encouragement:

Take time to invest in your spirit man. Develop strategies to encourage yourself on a daily basis. Give yourself a reason to be joyful and excited every day. You may experience some temporary setbacks, but when you do, bounce back. Tell of God's goodness so that others can come to the knowledge of Christ.

Life Lesson 10

After the Wilderness

After all has been said and done and your wilderness season is over, you can REJOICE! You made it through. Now, it's time to move on and enjoy a season of liberty. It's time to implement what you learned while you were in the wilderness. You took a stand against the enemy, you spoke the Word of God, you resisted the enemy, and you learned more about yourself during the wilderness season than you may have learned in a long time. You took control of your life and put old things and hindrances behind you. It's your time now to gain ground for Jesus.

When Jesus had overcome the temptations of the enemy, the Bible says, in Matthew 4:11, *"Then the devil leaveth him, and, behold, angels came and ministered unto him."* As I mentioned in an earlier chapter, the Father allowed Jesus to go through His wilderness season so that prophecy could be fulfilled. Then, after His trial was over, angels came and ministered to Him. This means they restored Him spiritually, physically and mentally (remember He was fully man and fully God). The mortal Jesus needed restoration after having endured the wilderness season. If Jesus needed to be ministered to, how much more do we need it?

Many times ministry comes through an encouraging word, a prayer, or some other type of motivation, to help you continue on your journey with God's help. Although the angels are there to encourage you, you also have a responsibility to encourage yourself. Make an effort on a daily basis to speak to yourself. Tell yourself, "You are blessed. You are victorious. You are healed." Whatever the need is, decree a blessing over your life, and then watch God bring it to pass. This daily activity may seem like spiritual calisthenics, but it will prove to be beneficial in the long run. When you practice encouraging yourself, you will be better equipped to stand when the enemy uses people or situations to try to tear you down.

Not only are we to speak the Word over our life daily, but we are also to clothe ourselves in the whole armor of God for divine protection. That armor consists of the helmet of salvation, the girdle of truth, the breastplate of righteousness, the shield of faith, good news shoes, and the sword of the Spirit (see the following verses). We have been given this armor so that we can be prepared for spiritual battle when wicked devices are launched against us.

The Bible tells us why this armor is needed and how to use it:

Ephesians 6:10-18

Finally, my brethren, be strong in the Lord, and in the power of his might. Put on the whole armour of God, that ye may be able to stand against the wiles of the devil. For we wrestle not against flesh and blood, but against principalities, against powers, against the rulers of the darkness of this world, against spiritual wickedness in high places. Wherefore take unto you the whole armour of God, that ye may be able to withstand in the evil day, and having done all, to stand.

Stand therefore, having your loins girt about with truth, and having on the breastplate of righteousness; and your feet shod with the preparation of the gospel of peace; above all, taking the shield of faith, wherewith ye shall be able to quench all the fiery darts of the wicked. And take the helmet of salvation, and the sword of the Spirit, which is the word of God. Praying always with all prayer and supplication in the Spirit, and watching thereunto with all perseverance and supplication for all saints.

We are destined for greatness because of the wealth of resources that God has provided for us in His Word. The Bible says:

After the Wilderness

2 Timothy 2:15

> *Study to shew thyself approved unto God, a workman that needeth not to be ashamed, rightly dividing the word of truth.*

The Bible itself teaches us the greatest lesson there is to learn, and it is that God's Word is *"a lamp unto [our] feet and a light unto [our] path"* (Psalm 119:105). His Word guides and directs us by teaching us how to live and overcome as believers.

I hope the life lessons I have shared with you in this book have helped you in some way to see your way clearer through the darkness of the wilderness. Galatians 5:1 states:

> *Stand fast therefore in the liberty wherewith Christ hath made us free, and be not entangled again with the yoke of bondage.*

You didn't have to do anything wrong to enter the wilderness season. It was a learning experience that taught you how to sustain yourself during every season of trial and overcome the enemy. As Christians, we should count it a privilege to have the opportunity to share our challenges and testimonies with others in order to lead them to Christ. I've enjoyed sharing with you as one of God's many messengers of the Good News.

LIFE LESSON 10
SELF CHECK

Have you ever been through something and you asked the Lord to just let you make it out of that situation and you would live right? Haven't we all? It's a good thing that we have new mercies every morning. We have another opportunity every day to start fresh. After the wilderness, you have so much more to offer to the Kingdom of God. God has set His seal of approval upon you.

Stop and Jot in your notebook!

What are you going to do next? Have you written down your vision? Great things are on the horizon. How will you impact your community and world around you? How are you preparing for God's next move?

Takeaways:

➤ Enjoy life!

➤ Expect God's best!

Encouragement:

It's your time to watch God move on your behalf like never before. Reach your highest potential. Share your testimony with someone. 1 Corinthians 2:9 says, *"But as it is written, Eye hath not seen, nor ear heard, neither have entered into the heart of man, the things which God hath prepared for them that love him."*

Author Contact Page

You may contact the author,
Stephanie S. Johnson, M.Ed.,
in the following ways:

Email: lifelessonsofthegoodteacher@gmail.com

Phone: 504-408-3591

www.ingramcontent.com/pod-product-compliance
Lightning Source LLC
LaVergne TN
LVHW022324080426
835508LV00041B/2539